COUNTRIES  OF THE WORLD

David Cumming

with photographs by Jimmy Holmes

Illustrated by Peter Bull

Titles in this series

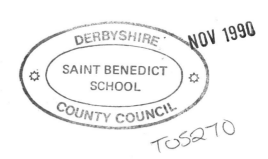

Australia	Italy
Canada	Japan
The Caribbean	The Netherlands
China	New Zealand
France	Pakistan
Great Britain	Spain
Greece	The U.S.A.
India	West Germany

Cover *A busy, bustling street in Madurai, south India.*

Opposite *Jaisalmer, in Rajasthan, is sometimes called the 'golden city' because many of the buildings are beautifully carved from golden-yellow sandstone.*

First published in 1989 by
Wayland (Publishers) Ltd
61 Western Road, Hove
East Sussex BN3 1JD, England

© Copyright 1989 Wayland (Publishers) Ltd

Series design: Malcolm Smythe
Book design: Force 9

British Library Cataloguing in Publication Data
Cumming, David
India.
1. India.
I. Title II. Holmes, Jimmy III. Series
954.05'2

ISBN 0-85078-966-4

Typeset by Oliver Dawkins Ltd., Burgess Hill, West Sussex
Printed in Italy by G. Canale and C.S.p.A., Turin
Bound in Belgium by Casterman S.A.

Contents

Words that appear in **bold** in the text are explained in the glossary on page 46.

1 Welcome to India

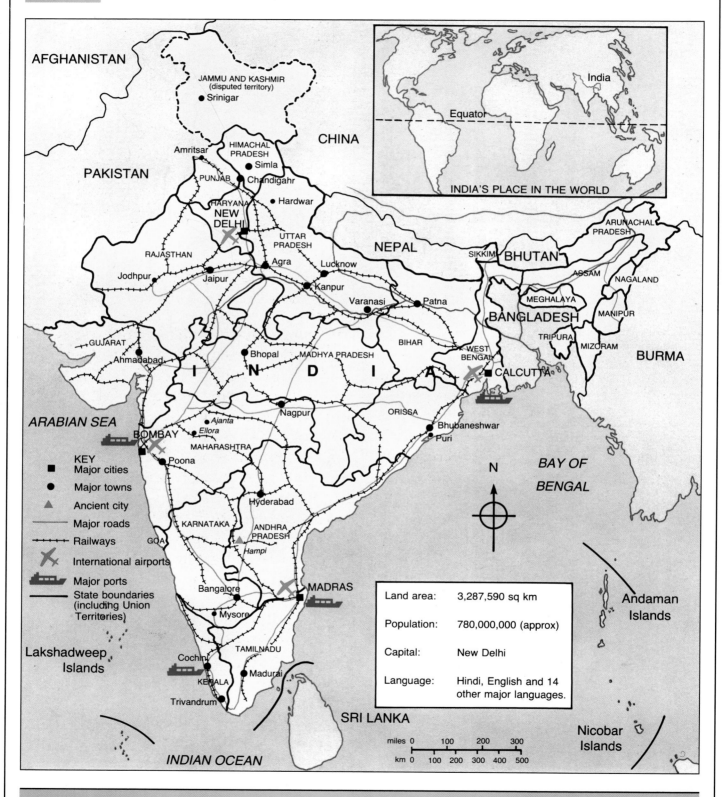

Land area: 3,287,590 sq km

Population: 780,000,000 (approx)

Capital: New Delhi

Language: Hindi, English and 14 other major languages.

KEY
- ■ Major cities
- ● Major towns
- ▲ Ancient city
- — Major roads
- +++ Railways
- ✕ International airports
- ⛴ Major ports
- — State boundaries (including Union Territories)

Flower-sellers in Jaipur; just some of the bright colours seen all over India.

Namaste! pronounced nam-ass-tay, is a Hindi greeting that is heard over much of India. It is a mixture of 'hallo' and 'how nice to see you'. You usually say it with the palms of your hands pressed together and your head slightly bowed, as a mark of respect to the person you are greeting. About 780 million people live in India, so can you imagine how many times *Namaste* is spoken each day?

India is north of the equator and shaped roughly like a triangle. To the west of it is Pakistan; to the east, Bangladesh and Burma; and to the north, Nepal and China. The Arabian Sea washes India's western shores; the Bay of Bengal, its eastern ones. The two meet at India's southernmost tip and become the Indian Ocean. The Andaman and Nicobar Islands in the Bay of Bengal, and the Lakshadweep Islands, in the Arabian Sea, are also part of India.

India is about 3,200 km from top to toe, and 2,900 km across at its widest point. It is the seventh largest country in the world: just over half the size of the USA and twice the size of Britain, France, West Germany and Italy put together. And its population is the second biggest after China's. In fact, every sixth person in the world is an Indian.

Throughout the 5,000 years of its known history, people have been attracted to India. Once it was to conquer the country. Today, people go to see the land that one of its rulers, Emperor Shah Jahan, called paradise on earth. Country is perhaps the wrong word to use to describe India, because it is more like a collection of mini-countries: each state has its own language, culture and customs, its own style of dress and way of cooking. There is differing scenery and wildlife, too.

2 Land and climate

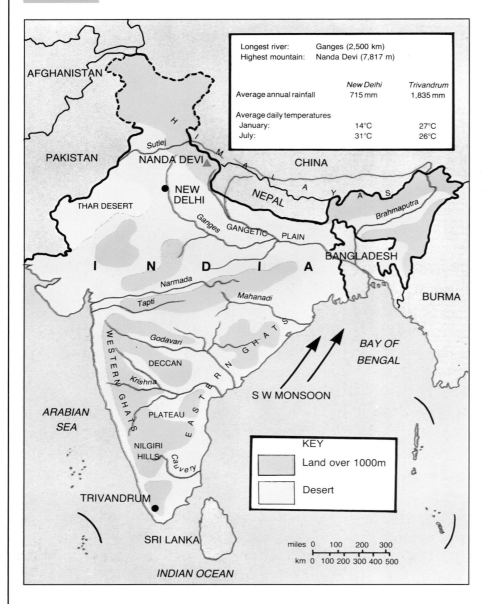

| Longest river: | Ganges (2,500 km) | |
| Highest mountain: | Nanda Devi (7,817 m) | |

	New Delhi	Trivandrum
Average annual rainfall	715 mm	1,835 mm
Average daily temperatures		
January:	14°C	27°C
July:	31°C	26°C

KEY

Land over 1000m

Desert

Above *A fishing village in south India. This region has a tropical climate, so it is hot all year round.*

High above us, satellites made in India are circling the earth, sending scientists information on the land and weather beneath them. What do their pictures of India show?

They reveal a landscape of **contrasts**: from high mountains to flat plains; from dusty deserts to soggy swamps and from sandy beaches to thick forests. Despite this variety, we can divide India into three main areas.

The Himalayas stretch for 2,400 km across the north of the country. They are a massive and imposing wall of snow and ice, with some of the highest mountains in the world.

South of the mountains, stretching right across the middle of India, are the flat plains along the River Ganges. This land is good for farming food crops, especially wheat. And with plenty of food available, people have moved here in large numbers. Now two out of every three Indians live on the plains.

South of the plains the land rises again to the Deccan Plateau, the dry region of the pointed peninsula of southern India. Either side of it are mountain ranges, with slopes covered in forests and plantations where coffee and tea are grown.

Between the mountains and the sea is a strip of land where coconuts, bananas and spices are cultivated. Down here, people can go swimming in the warm oceans while those further north are wrapped up in their winter coats. This is because the south is nearer the equator, so it is always hot. Being further away from the equator, the plains have hot summers, but cool winters.

In the summer, the **monsoon** winds bring rain to all of India. Although vital for thirsty crops, the rain comes very suddenly and can cause floods that can devastate the land. Some Indian cities receive more rain in a couple of months than falls on San Francisco or London in a whole year. In some years the monsoon does not bring enough rain and the crops die. Now India's satellites are helping to predict how much rain will fall.

Above *The Thar Desert, in Rajasthan, is one of the driest parts of India.*

Right *A fertile mountain valley in Kashmir. Much of northern India is mountainous.*

3 Wildlife

Each animal and bird has its own habitat, which is the type of place where it likes to live. With mountains, jungles, deserts and plains, India has so many types of habitat that a large variety of animals live there. In the hills and mountains there are tigers, bears and falcons. Peacocks, camels, lizards and deadly snakes live on the plains. There are monkeys, leopards and elephants in the jungles and crocodiles in the rivers.

There used to be many tigers in India, but hunters have killed many of them for their precious skins.

Sadly, hunting has been common in India for a long time. It was important for food and for money. Animal skins and horns can still fetch a good price today. Hunting for sport was also common, especially by the British when they ruled India. The hunters killed so many animals that some were in danger of being wiped out altogether. To stop this, the government has banned the hunting of certain **species**, including the tiger and the one-horned rhinoceros, and set up special parks where they can now live in safety.

Left The peacock is one of the 2,000 species of birds to be found in India.

Below A wild Indian elephant in Madumalai Wildlife Reserve in Tamil Nadu, southern India.

India's animals have also been harmed by people chopping down trees for firewood. This has destroyed many forests and forced animals to live on the plains, where it is easier for other animals and humans to kill them.

Since tree roots keep the soil together, destroying forests has also meant that good farming soil has been washed away by the monsoon rains. Now the government is stopping people cutting down trees to protect both the soil and the animals.

India's religions have always taught their followers to respect animals and not to harm them. In the **Hindu** religion, cows are **sacred** because they provide milk, so Hindus will not kill them. Members of one small and ancient Hindu sect, called Jains, wear a mask over their mouths to prevent them swallowing insects. This is because they respect all life as sacred.

Times past

Most of the people from whom modern-day Indians are descended migrated to India from other parts of the world. About 5,000 years ago, there were people who lived near the rivers in the north.

Around 1500 BC, they were conquered by the **Aryans** from Europe, who named the Indian people **Dravidians**. The Aryans stayed in northern India to rule over the Dravidians, many of whom fled to the south. Under the Aryans, the Hindu religion developed.

Descendants of the Aryans remained powerful until the **Moguls** from central Asia overthrew them in AD 1526. Like the Aryans, the Moguls settled in the north, leaving the south to itself. The Moguls followed the **Islamic** religion, which replaced Hinduism as the main religion in the north. During the reign of the greatest Mogul, Akbar, traders from Europe began arriving.

In 1611, Britain opened its first trading post. It was run by the East India Company, which soon became very powerful, even having its own army. As the British expanded, so the Mogul empire began to break up. The British occupation was opposed by many Indians, who saw them using their country to make the British Empire wealthier at their expense, taking over more and more of their land.

In 1857 there was a big **mutiny** by Indian soldiers in the East India Company's army. The British government felt threatened and decided

An old painting of the great Mogul Emperor, Akbar, crossing the River Ganges with his soldiers.

it was time to seize power over the whole of India. The Indians remained restless under British rule. By the 1920s, those who wanted the end of British rule had found a new leader, Mahatma Gandhi. Mahatma Gandhi believed in self-government for the Indian people. He persuaded thousands of Indians to take part in non-violent actions to force out the British.

The Taj Mahal, near Agra, is one of the most beautiful buildings in the world. It was built by Emperor Shah Jahan in memory of his wife, Mumtaz Mahal, after her death. It took 21 years to build, from 1632 to 1653.

Unfortunately, Gandhi and the other Hindu leaders could not agree with the **Muslim** leaders on how India should be governed. In 1947 the British left India, splitting the country into Muslim and Hindu areas. West Pakistan (now Pakistan) and East Pakistan (now Bangladesh) were created for Muslims.

The remainder was a mainly Hindu country, which is the India we know today.

Although India became **independent** in 1947, it still remained a part of the **Commonwealth**. On 26 January 1950 India became a **democratic republic** within the Commonwealth.

Important dates		
3000 BC	People living in northern India.	
1500 BC	Aryans invade India.	
273-232	Emperor Ashoka rules a vast empire in northern India, with Hinduism as its main religion.	
AD 1498	The Portuguese explorer, Vasco da Gama, sails around Africa and reaches India, opening up a trading route with Europe.	
1526	Battle of Panipat (near Delhi). Babur becomes the first Mogul emperor. Islam is the religion of his empire.	
1556-1605	Emperor Akbar reigns.	
1600	East India Company set up by Queen Elizabeth I of England.	
1611	First East India Company trading post opens in India.	
1857	Indian Mutiny.	
1878	Queen Victoria becomes Empress of India.	
1947	India becomes independent from British rule.	
1950	India becomes a democratic republic.	
1952	Nehru becomes India's first prime minister.	
1971	India at war with Pakistan. Bangladesh gains independence.	
1984	Indira Gandhi, Nehru's daughter and India's first woman prime minister, assassinated. Her son, Rajiv Gandhi, takes her place.	

5 Religion

Hindus bathing in the holy River Ganges at one of the ghats in Varanasi.

Today, 8 out of 10 Indian people are Hindus. Hindus believe in a kind of fate — that it has already been decided what your life will be like and nothing you do can change it. They worship many different gods and a supreme being called Brahma. They also believe in reincarnation. That means that when you die your soul is born again in another body. Connected with this idea is the '**caste**' system.

Caste is the term for the four inherited Hindu social classes. The most important caste are the *Brahmins*, who are the priests, followed by the *Kshastrias, Vaisayas* and *Sudras*. There is a social group who have no caste, who are called the *Harijans*. Hindus believe that if you live a good life, then you will be reborn into a higher caste. The caste system is still important in the countryside, but less so in the cities.

Religions	Followers (approx)
Hinduism	624,000,000
Islam	86,000,000
Christianity	20,250,000
Sikhism	14,750,000
Buddhism	5,500,000
Jews, Jains, Parsees	6,250,000

Left The Jama Masjid in Old Delhi. It is the largest mosque in India – 25,000 Muslims can worship in it at one time.

Below A huge temple 'car' being pulled through the streets of Udipi during a festival for the god Krishna.

Hindus celebrate the births and deaths of important people in their religion's history with colourful and exciting festivals. One of the most spectacular is called the *Kumbh Mela*, when over one million people travel to Hardwar to bathe in the River Ganges, which is thought to be the most sacred river in India. In Puri, on the east coast, a similar number come to watch the statue of the god Jagannath being pulled around the city in a gigantic chariot.

After Hinduism, Islam is the most important religion. About 1 in every 10 people is a Muslim (the name of its followers). They have one god called Allah. In the Punjab, Sikhism is the main religion. Sikhs believe there is only one god and that people should spend their lives serving him. There are also Parsees, found mainly in western India, Christians, **Buddhists** and Jews.

6 People and language

Ask anyone who has been to India what they remember most about their visit. The heat? The scenery? The food? Many people will answer: the crowds. In the cities, India seems to be bursting at the seams with people — narrow streets are chock-a-block with them; train carriages crammed full with them; buses overflowing with them.

They are all Indians, but they do not all look or dress the same. In the cities, many men and women wear Western-type clothes. In the country areas, people tend to wear more traditional styles.

The *sari*, usually worn over a short-sleeved blouse, is the popular form of dress for women in India. It is a long piece of colourful cloth that is wound round the body and draped over one shoulder. But in central India, it is usually wrapped around the waist and tucked between the legs. In the hot south, women just wrap the cloth around their waist, like a long skirt. This is called a *lunghi*, which is also worn by men since it is a very cool way of dressing.

Above A family from Bombay. The sari, a long piece of coloured cotton, is worn by women all over India. This woman's husband and children are wearing Western-type clothes, which is common in India's larger cities.

Left A travelling family in Rajasthan. Most Rajasthani men wear brightly coloured turbans. The women often wear jewellery and clothes embroidered with silk or gold thread.

Above *Traditionally-dressed women from a remote northern area of Himachal Pradesh.*

Above *This south Indian man is paddling his bamboo raft in a cool lunghi.*

The *dhoti* is worn by men all over the country, but especially in the eastern state of Bengal. It is a long, wide length of white cotton that is wrapped around the waist, with the end pulled up and tucked between the legs. In north-western India, men wear tight-fitting long jackets and trousers, as do the women, but with blouses instead of jackets.

In any crowd of Indians, you can easily recognize males of the **Sikh** religion from Punjab state by the **turbans** they wear around their heads. Men from Rajasthan state wear similar turbans, but they are usually more colourful.

Right *Sikh men wear a turban for religious reasons. Sikh women usually wear trousers with a tunic over the top.*

Not only do Indians differ in appearance, they also speak different languages. Those spoken in southern India originated from the earliest people, the Dravidians. The languages of the north come from those brought by the Aryans when they conquered India. Having different languages means that many northerners and southerners cannot communicate with each other.

When the British ruled India, they made English the language for business and government matters, and encouraged all Indians to learn it. As a result, India is now the second largest English-speaking nation in the world.

Above *A street corner in Calcutta. The hoardings are printed in several languages, including Bengali, Hindi and English.*

After India gained its independence in 1947, it was split up into different states according to the language of each area, so that all the people in one state spoke the same language. To make it easier for each state to communicate with another, it was decided that Hindi, the main northern language, should become the language spoken throughout India. English was to continue as the second language while everyone was learning to speak Hindi.

Naturally, the people who spoke the other languages did not like this idea and refused to learn Hindi. So, today, although half of the population can speak Hindi, probably more people speak English. Now, besides Hindi and English, there are fourteen other main languages spoken around India as well as hundreds of local **dialects**.

Above *A collection of Indian notes, coins and stamps. They are printed in Hindi and English.*

This fortune-teller's signs are written in Malayalam, an important language of southern India.

Left This man is a potter. His wife and children help him in the family business. Pottery is still a very important small-scale industry all over India.

To complicate things even more, India's languages are not all written in the same way. For instance, the four main languages of the south (Telugu, Kanada, Tamil and Malayalam) are written in a different style to Hindi.

Although there are many differences in the appearance, speech and lifestyles of people in India, one thing that most Indians have in common is the importance of their family. Indian families are often large and they believe in helping each other. Several generations—grandparents, parents and children—may all share the same home. They will not only eat together but often work together too.

7 Cities

If you were flying in a helicopter and looked down on an Indian city, you would see that it is divided up into areas. From these it is possible to see the different stages of India's history.

To start with, most Indian cities have an old part, with a fort and the remains of the wall that once surrounded it. Perhaps the wall once kept out the armies of an attacking Mogul emperor. Within the wall, there will be a maze of narrow streets and alley-ways, full of open-fronted shops and bustling **bazaars**.

Above The old fort in the ancient walled city of Jaisalmer in Rajasthan.

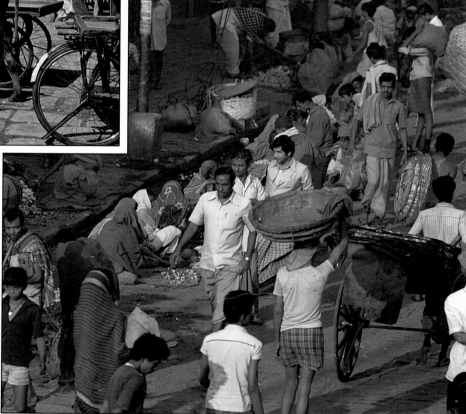

Right Bow Bazaar, a busy street in the centre of Calcutta.

Several kilometres away will be the area where the British built their homes, hospitals and army barracks. Here, there are wide, straight roads with trees on either side, and a railway station. Between this part and the old city are the government offices that were built by the British.

Off one of the main roads leading into the city, an industrial estate of factories will have developed; off another, a modern area with high-rise blocks of flats and houses near shops. Far on the outskirts there may be an airport.

India's three main cities, Delhi, Calcutta and Bombay, have most of these areas. Delhi, with a population of 6 million, is the capital and home of the government and parliament. Its 'old city' is crammed with markets, shops and temples. The new part, built by the British in the 1930s, has tree-lined avenues of large houses, many now in the shadows of multi-storey hotels and office blocks.

The largest city in India is Calcutta, with 9 million people. This city is famous for its artists, writers and dancers. At its centre is the *Maidan*, an enormous park with cricket pitches and football fields.

Once a fishing village, Bombay is now India's main port, and the centre of India's thriving film industry. There are many other important industries here, including polishing precious stones, such as diamonds.

Above *A new high-rise office block in Connaught Place, in the heart of New Delhi.*

Right *A woman selling fish in Bombay's docks. Bombay is the main port of India.*

8 Country life

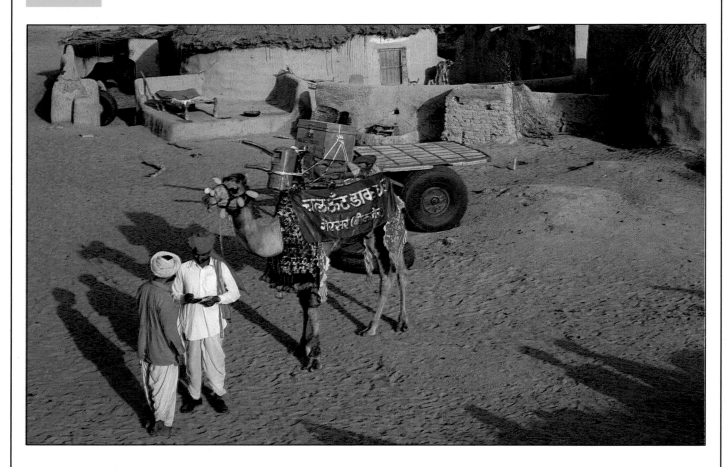

In the Thar Desert, the postman travels between settlements by camel.

Most Indians live in the countryside. Out of every five people, four live in small villages, far away from the cities, railways and main roads.

Most of these people are farmers. The seasons play an important part in their lives, with sowing and harvesting being the busiest times. These farmers work very hard, yet many are very poor. At the end of the year, they may seem to be no better off than at the start.

The main reason for this is that many farmers do not own the land on which they work. They have to pay rent for its use to the owners. Since they have hardly any money, the farmers pay the landowner in kind: that is, by giving him a share of their harvest.

If the harvest has been poor, perhaps because the monsoon has brought little rain or because pests have damaged the crop, the farmer still has to give the landowner his share. Often this means that the farmer ends up with just enough to feed his family, with nothing to sell for money to buy things like cooking oil and flour.

As the farmer cannot save, he may have to borrow money from a money-lender, at very high interest rates — sometimes as much as 100 per cent. This means that for every rupee borrowed, 2 rupees will have to be paid back. After several bad harvests, a farmer may have a large debt with the money-lender.

Villagers who live on the coast may be fishermen. Those that are not farmers or fishermen may make the everyday goods that their village needs, such as tools, cooking pots and clothes. Some villagers move to a city to look for work. If they find a job they will send home money to help support their family.

When villagers are not working, time is spent with friends and relatives, celebrating religious festivals or family occasions, like birthdays and marriages.

Above Indian farmers work very hard. This farmer, in Kerala state, is preparing a paddyfield. Rice is the main crop of the south.

Below The first snows of winter covering a village in Kashmir, at the foot of the Himalayan Mountains.

9 Growing up in a village

A typical village may consist of some 200 homes, made of stone, brick or mud, surrounded by fields. The homes will have two or three small rooms, all with an earthen floor. In many families there are parents, young children, perhaps a married elder son, and uncles and aunts or grandparents. The family lives simply.

Left A young girl looking after her family's buffaloes in northern India.

Below Villagers drying cow dung. This will later be used as an inexpensive fuel for fires on which the family's food can be cooked.

Many villagers can catch a bus, like this one, to their nearest town.

Much of the time will be spent in the courtyard outside, where meals are cooked over a cow-dung fire and the family's animals are tied up.

Work takes up most of the time in the country and, when they are old enough, children are expected to lend a hand. Traditionally, girls help their mothers with the chores of running a home, doing things like fetching water from the well and preparing meals. Their brothers will look after the animals or help their father in the fields.

Children will be sent to the village school at the age of 5 or 6. If the village is near a town, the boys will then go to the secondary school there, when they are 10. Girls sometimes stay at home and then marry when they are about 16 to a boy chosen by their parents. When boys finish school, the elder son will probably stay to help his father, while his younger brothers go off to a city or town to work.

10 Growing up in a city

Life is very different in the city. Many city children will live in a small flat in a tower block, with their parents and several other relations. The flat will have running water, electricity and gas for cooking, but often little furniture. The father of the family will probably own a scooter, on which he will go to work and also take his children to school in the morning.

Children of wealthy parents live in large houses. They may have large rooms, lots of comfortable furniture, a telephone, television and video, and a fitted kitchen and bathroom. In the drive outside will be a car. There may be a chauffeur who will look after the car and also the large garden. The children will have lots of smart clothes and go to a private school. At weekends, they will have enough money to go to the cinema and then buy a hamburger at one of the many take-aways opening up in Indian cities.

Children attending a modern school in New Delhi.

Left *Part of a shanty town on the outskirts of New Delhi.*

Sadly, some of the young people who move to the cities looking for work end up living on the streets. Finding a job is difficult, so many roam the streets, forced to beg and steal to survive. Home for many of them is a blanket in a shop entrance. And there is no one to make them go to school.

There is plenty to see and do in Indian cities. This typically busy street scene is in Lucknow, a city in northern India.

Others end up staying in one of the **shanty towns** on the outskirts, living in a shack made out of bits of wood, tin and cardboard. The shacks have no running water or electricity and are often flooded by the monsoon rains. Shanty towns have developed because there are not enough homes in the cities for the people who have left the countryside. As more people are moving to work in the cities' factories, the problem is getting worse, although the government is trying to deal with the problem.

Apart from those with no homes, city children are generally better provided for than the children living in India's 600,000 villages. There is also more for them to see and do, such as visiting museums, zoos and sports grounds.

11 Education

The day begins at a school, run by the government, in south India.

In India, less than half the population is able to read or write. One reason for this is that most of the schools and colleges are in the cities, a long way from the villages where most of the people live. Another reason is that, even though schools run by the government are free, most families are poor and their children have to start earning money as soon as they can, so they are not sent to school.

Some parents send only their sons to school, because they know that a good education will help their sons to find work, whereas it is traditional for daughters to stay at home.

Governments have tried to make things better by building more schools so that every child can be taught until they are 14 years old. This has been possible in Kerala state, where 8 out of 10 people can now read and write.

Country children may have three or four years at their village school. Some villages have no school building and lessons may be held using a blackboard under a large tree. A village that has been able to afford a television or transistor radio can make use of the special school programmes that are now broadcast.

In a city, a child receives a better education. He or she will be able to go to a primary school, then a secondary school and perhaps on to a college or university.

Many village schools hold classes in the open air.

Below *A bookstall in Kerala state, where 8 out of 10 people can read and write.*

12 Food and drink

Mention Indian food and many people tend to think of fiery, spicy curries. In fact, the word 'curry' was introduced by the British to describe the spicyness of all Indian food and not just one particular dish. As you would expect in a country of India's size, there is a great variety of food and many different ways of cooking it.

Many Indian dishes are vegetarian. These will be just spicy enough to be tasty. Every housewife has her own special mixture of spices for the dishes she cooks, but the commonly used ones include turmeric, ginger, garlic, coriander and cloves. In the north, where a lot of wheat is farmed, food will be accompanied by *nan* or *chapatis* (flat breads). In the south, the rice-growing part of India, you are more likely to be served rice with your meal.

Most Indians do not eat with knives and forks. Instead, they roll the food up into little balls with their right hand and pop them into their mouths. Food is often eaten off a *thali*, a metal tray on which little bowls of different dishes are placed, along with pickles and chutneys. In the south, banana leaves are often used as plates.

Above left *Many Indian men chew pan – betel nuts, lime and spices wrapped up in a leaf from the betel tree.*

Left *Indians will buy spices for their food from a stall like this one.*

Above In the south, people often eat their food off banana leaves, which they throw away afterwards.

Water will be drunk with the meal. Indians also like sweet, soft drinks or tea. Tea is made by putting the water, tea leaves, milk and sugar into one saucepan and boiling them up, perhaps with a spice, like cardamon, added. In the south, more coffee is drunk than tea.

Wherever you go in India the streets will be lined with stalls selling all kinds of mouth-watering snacks.

Fresh vegetables for sale at a market in Jaipur.

13 Leisure and pleasure

India is a sports-loving nation and the open spaces in its cities and villages are full of people playing team games. Cricket is the sport for which India is most famous and everyone is proud of their national team. Matches between India and other countries fill every seat in the cricket ground. Every radio and television set around the country seems to be tuned into the game as Indians excitedly follow their team's progress.

Hockey is another sport for which India is famous, and Indian teams have won many gold medals in the Olympic Games.

Above Polo being played on a pitch in the city of Leh, in Ladakh, high up in the Himalayan Mountains.

Below Many Indians enjoy going to the cinema. The Indian film industry is one of the biggest in the world.

In the cities, there is a wide choice of activities to take part in and watch. Many cities now have modern sports stadiums which are well equipped for both indoor and outdoor activities. In Calcutta, Bombay and Poona, there are horse-racing tracks where many of the wealthier Indians go to watch the racing and gamble. Many of these people will also be seen on the golf courses around most cities. In winter, they may go up to Narkanda, in northern India, to ski.

In the country, football or cricket is played. Children play games, like *guli danda*, where they take it in turns to hit a small piece of wood with a stick to make it spin up in the air. Then they try to hit it again and send it as far as they can.

Aside from sports, a favourite pastime is going to the cinema. In the country, a travelling cinema van will visit villages to give open-air film shows.

A family outing to the ruins of the ancient city of Hampi. This beautiful stone chariot was carved in the fifteenth century, when Hampi was the capital of an enormous empire.

In the evenings, most people stay at home or perhaps visit their friends or relatives. There are no bars or discos in the cities and only the rich go out to restaurants. Villagers may play cards and chat with their friends at the end of the day.

Every Sunday, cricket matches are played in this large park in Bombay.

14 The Arts

From the beautiful wall paintings and rock carvings in the temple caves at Ajanta and Ellora, inland from Bombay, we know that very skilled artists and sculptors were at work in India at least two thousand years ago.

Their descendants built magnificent temples all over India, which were covered from top to bottom with detailed carvings of gods and goddesses. Their interiors were often decorated with statues, made out of bronze and precious metals by craftsmen in southern India.

When people went to pray at these temples, they would find dancers acting out religious stories. Temple dancers can no longer be seen, but Indian dancers still perform at festivals in the way they did all those hundreds of years ago.

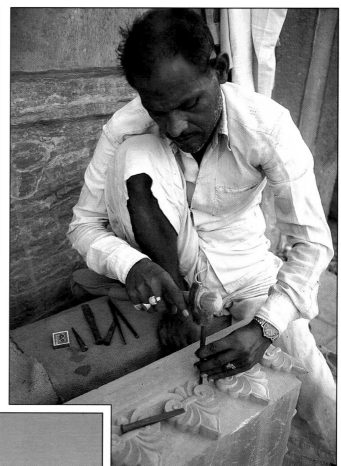

Above Stonemasons, like this man, have been practising their art in India for thousands of years.

Left A concert hall in Madras, India's fourth largest city.

The Mogul rulers of India brought new styles of building, the most famous example of which is the Taj Mahal, with its dome, spires and arches of marble. The Moguls also encouraged artists to paint very small pictures, full of detail and brightly coloured. In many parts of India, artists still specialize in this type of miniature painting with the skills handed down over generations.

Right Kathakali dancers in Kerala state. The origins of the dance can be traced back 2,000 years.

A miniature painting showing a scene from the famous Indian poem, the Ramayana.

Literature has long been a part of Indian culture, too. Two of the most famous books are the *Mahabharata* and the *Ramayana*. They are both long poems, which were written two thousand years ago. Much poetry is still written in India, especially in the state of Bengal. One of the greatest Indian poets of this century was a Bengali, named Rabindranath Tagore (who also wrote the Indian national anthem). He has won a **Nobel prize** for his work.

Indians have developed a thriving film industry. Satyajit Ray, another Bengali, has brought India fame around the world with his skills as a film maker. His films have won many awards.

15 Farming

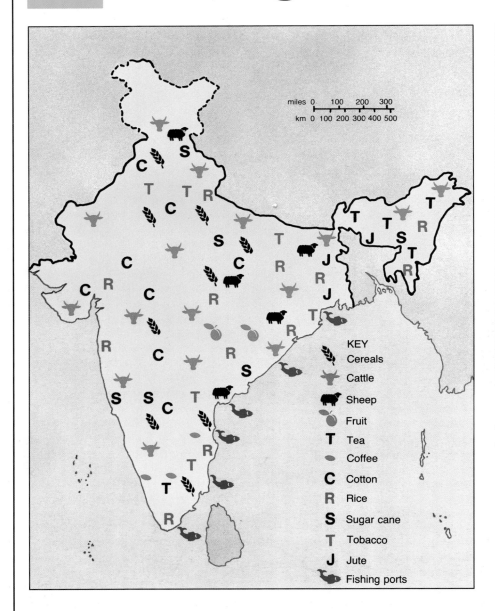

Taking in the harvest near Srinigar, Kashmir. This crop has been cut by hand.

KEY

Cereals	
Cattle	
Sheep	
Fruit	
T	Tea
	Coffee
C	Cotton
R	Rice
S	Sugar cane
T	Tobacco
J	Jute
	Fishing ports

Most of India's farmland is used to grow crops for food. Farming is also important because it provides jobs for nearly three-quarters of India's workers.

Indians eat a lot of rice and wheat, so these are the main crops grown. Rice is cultivated along the wetter coastal areas. Wheat is farmed on the flat, drier plains in the north, especially in the state of Punjab. Other important food crops are sugar cane and pulses (peas, beans and lentils).

Most of the farmers farm using the simple methods that have been passed down through the years. They are often too poor to buy fertilizers and farm machinery. Even if they had more money, most of the farms are too small to make it worthwhile to use a large machine like a tractor. They plough, sow and harvest by hand, with the help of an ox or bullock to pull a plough or a cart.

The weather is another problem, since the monsoons are unreliable and sometimes bring too little rain. Pests, too, can damage crops.

The government has improved things by encouraging farmers to join their lands together into bigger farms and by providing money to dig wells and buy machines, fertilizers and seeds that produce better, more disease-resistant crops. These have dramatically increased food supplies and helped to relieve some of the rural poverty. It has been called the 'Green Revolution'.

Indian farmers also grow crops to sell to factories and to other countries. The main export crops are tea and jute, which is used to make ropes and sacks, and cotton for clothing factories.

Below *Tea being picked on a hillside plantation in southern India.*

16 Industry

A Sikh family in the Punjab printing cloth with vegetable dyes, using hand blocks.

Most of the people who are not farmers are involved in making things. In India, these people work in either very large factories or small workshops.

Workshops, often run by members of the same family, have been part of the Indian way of life for hundreds of years, long before its cities and factories were built. Many articles are made, such as beautifully carved furniture, gleaming silver, brass bowls, carefully woven carpets, rugs and material for clothes.

These workshops still exist, and they have been joined by others, where such things as radios, table lamps and kitchen equipment are made. Together, these small businesses produce half of everything made by all of India's industries.

The most important industrial area is near Calcutta, in the Damodar valley. It is a prime example of one of India's most successful multi-purpose development plans. Its factories make iron and steel, cement, machines for other factories, chemicals and textiles. Industrialization on this scale has been made possible with financial help from richer nations.

The factories were built in the Damodar valley because many minerals, including iron ore, copper and bauxite, are in the ground nearby. India has many millions of tonnes of minerals in the earth, waiting to be dug up. This means that it does not have to buy a lot of them from other countries.

But minerals are of no use unless they can be changed into a metal, which can then be shaped by a machine. Heat and electricity are needed for these processes. In the Damodar valley, the heat is provided by coal and the electricity by **hydroelectric power**. India uses a lot of both to provide power for its factories and homes. Gas, oil and nuclear energy are also used to supply power to India's cities and industries.

Above The Hirakud Dam, in Orissa, is used to irrigate farmland as well as supply hydro-electric power.

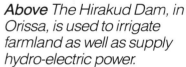

Left An open-cast iron ore mine in Goa state, on India's west coast.

Main exports:	Crude oil, handicrafts, clothing, tea, precious stones
Main imports:	Petroleum, machinery, precious stones, chemicals, fertilizers

17 Transport

India has more bullock carts than cars: for every car, there are 12 carts. Perhaps this is not surprising when we remember that India is a nation of farmers—a bullock is more useful to them as it can be used to plough fields as well as pull a cart to the market.

In the countryside, you will also see *tongas* (horse-drawn carts) full of people and their luggage. In the desert regions of Rajasthan state, camels are used to pull the carts.

These carts will also be seen in the cities, squeezed between honking cars, noisy scooters and motor bikes, three-wheeled pedal and motorized rickshaws, and buses.

River craft on the River Hooghly, which connects Calcutta to the sea.

Above *Some of India's many types of transport.*

India's cities are connected by road, rail and air. By road, people can travel by bus or comfortable coaches, many of them with aircraft-type seats, air-conditioning and videos showing films. But most Indians use the vast network of trains to travel between cities.

Every day, 10 million people travel by train. The first route was opened in 1853. Today, with 61,000 km of track, it is the largest railway system in the whole of Asia and the second largest in the world. Even by train, travelling across India takes a long time: Calcutta, in the east, to Bombay, in the west, takes 36 hours; from Delhi, in the north, to Trivandrum, at the southern tip, takes 48 hours. Many trains have **buffet cars**, and seats that convert into bunk beds at night; some have air-conditioned carriages to keep passengers cool.

Of course, it is much quicker to fly, for those who can afford to do so. Within India, the planes of Indian Airlines can reach even the most out-of-the-way places in a matter of hours. Air India, the international airline, flies all over the world.

A train waits at the station while the guard has a drink. Ten million people travel on India's trains every day. It is one of the largest rail systems in the world.

18 Health

Large, modern hospitals, like this one, are helping Indians to lead a healthier, longer life.

At independence, in 1947, most Indians did not live much longer than their early thirties. Now, most can expect to live almost twice as long.

One reason for this is that there are more doctors and hospitals, which means that more people can be treated for illnesses, and given injections and pills to stop them catching diseases. As a result, smallpox, which used to kill thousands, has been stamped out. Other dangerous diseases, like cholera and malaria, still exist, but far fewer people are dying of them. New drugs developed in the West, and assistance from the World Health Organization, have also helped.

The government has also been telling people how these diseases are caused and how they can prevent themselves from catching them. Most of them are spread by dirty drinking water, so cities now add chemicals to their water to destroy the germs.

As well as being better protected from diseases, Indians are much healthier than they were in the 1940s. Doctors have been training health workers about the best types of food to eat so that the body gets enough vitamins. They have then travelled around the cities and villages telling people how to look after themselves. Today, Indians, especially children and babies, are fitter and catch fewer illnesses.

But, by making India a healthier place, another problem has been created: India now has a population that is getting bigger day by day. Millions of Indians are alive today who 30 or 40 years ago would have died before becoming adults. Now they are watching their own children grow up.

Above A small rural hospital in Kerala.

Below A Sikh dentist attends to a patient on a roadside pavement.

Above Filling water pots at the village tap. Clean water is essential in preventing the spread of disease.

The government is trying to slow down the increase in the number of babies being born by advising parents to have only two children. Otherwise, if the population continues to grow at its present rate, there will be 1,000 million people in India by the year 2000.

19 Government

India's government is split up into states and union territories. In each of these, most people speak the same language and have the same customs. Ideally these areas can look after themselves, yet still feel part of India.

The states are like mini-countries, each with their own capital, government and parliament for making laws. The members of the parliament are chosen in elections by the citizens of the states.

Above *Rajiv Gandhi (in the grey suit) is India's Prime Minister and the leader of the Congress Party. Here he is representing India at an international conference.*

Below *Part of the spectacular procession held every 26 January in New Delhi to celebrate the day India became a republic.*

The union territories do not have a governor or parliament, but are run from the capital city, Delhi.

In Delhi, there is a national parliament that decides how India as a whole should work, but it lets the state parliament put these decisions into practice. The Delhi parliament is made up of two houses: the *Rajya Sabha* (meaning Council of States) and the *Lok Sabha* (meaning House of the People).

The *Rajya Sabha* has 250 members, who come from each state's parliament. This means that all the states have a say in how India is run.

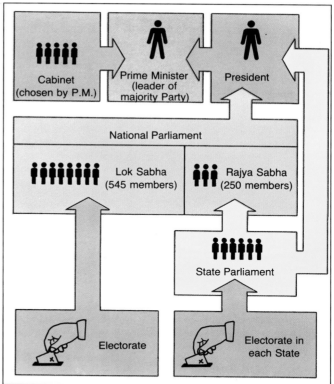

Above *The structure of the Indian government.*

The *Lok Sabha* has 545 members. These are chosen every five years. All Indians over 21 years of age can vote at elections. The party that has the most members selects the prime minister, who runs India with the help of parliament and a cabinet of ministers.

Above the prime minister is the president of India, who is chosen by both the Delhi parliament and the state parliaments. The president makes sure that the government and the parliaments behave according to the Indian constitution, which are the rules that have been written down to say how India should be run.

A notice-board showing the results of voting in elections for the Lok Sabha.

20 Facing the future

Left The Golden Temple in Amritsar, the Sikh's holiest shrine and the scene of battles between the army and Sikhs seeking independence from India.

Below A hoarding advising Indian parents to have small families.

In the years since it became independent, India has solved a great many problems, but some still exist and will take many years to sort out.

The most important one is India's growing population — more than one million babies are born every month. Eventually, they will need homes and jobs. These are already difficult to find, especially in the crowded cities, but they will become even more difficult to find when there are more people looking for them.

One of the reasons Indians tend to have large families is because they believe that the more children they have, the more people there will be to earn money for the family and to look after them when they are old. Some people say that if Indians were richer, they would not need large families. But providing ways for the poor to earn more money will be a long and difficult task.

Another problem is that some states think the government in Delhi makes them do things that may be good for India, but not for them. They would prefer to become independent countries and look after their own affairs. The Sikhs, for example, want to make Punjab state into a country called Khalistan. The government is against this since it thinks that India should not be split into many different countries.

The relationship between India and Pakistan is another concern. There have been troubles between some of the Hindus and the Muslims. They have argued over who should own Kashmir. This has caused two wars and the matter is still not settled. In 1971, the two countries went to war again, when India supported Bangladesh in its fight for independence. Let us hope that the two countries will one day be at peace.

In the last thirty years, health and education have improved, the 'Green Revolution' has helped India to double the amount of food produced, and advances in industrial development and technology have boosted the economy and raised standards of living. India still faces many challenges, but both the government and the people are working hard and making progress.

What lies ahead for this child in south India?

Glossary

Aryans The people who invaded northern India around 1500 BC.

Bazaar A market area, often a street with many small stalls.

Buddhists Followers of the Buddhist faith, which began in India.

Buffet car A railway coach where light refreshments are served.

Caste The term for the inherited social divisions in the Hindu faith.

Commonwealth The association of states that are, or have at some time been, ruled by Britain.

Contrast A clear difference between things.

Democratic republic A system of government by representatives elected by the people (instead of being governed by a king, queen or emperor).

Dialects A way of speaking used in a particular part of a country, or used by a particular group of people.

Dravidians The earliest inhabitants of India. Many of them escaped to southern India after the Aryans arrived.

Hindus The followers of one of the main religions of India, Hinduism. It was originally brought to India by the Aryans.

Hydroelectric power (HEP) Using water power to make electricity.

Islam A Middle Eastern religion brought to India by Arab traders and the Moguls.

Independent Being free from the control of others (for example, when a country stops being ruled by foreigners). India became independent in 1947 when the British left.

Moguls The people who began invading India in AD 1398.

Monsoon A strong wind which blows over the Indian Ocean in the summer, bringing rain. It is also used to describe the heavy rains.

Muslim Followers of the Islamic faith.

Mutiny A rebellion by soldiers and sailors against their officers.

Nobel prize An annual international prize awarded for making an outstanding contribution to society.

Sacred Something holy or of religious significance.

Sikhs Followers of the Sikh religion, that began in north-west India.

Species A group of animals or plants that are similar (for example, lions and tigers are both species of cat).

Shanty town A collection of homes, made out of any materials found by their inhabitants, such as corrugated iron or cardboard.

Turban A type of hat worn by men. It is made by wrapping a long strip of cloth around the head.

Books to read

Ahsan, M.M.   *Muslim Festivals* (Wayland, 1985)

Arora, Ranjit   *Sikhism* (Wayland, 1986)

Bahree, Patricia   *The Hindu World* (Macdonald, 1982)

Blackwood, Alan   *Asoka and Ancient India* (Wayland, 1986)

Douglas, Gina   *The Ganges* (Wayland, 1978)

Hargreaves, Pat   *The Indian Ocean* (Wayland, 1981)

Hunter, Nigel   *Gandhi* (Wayland, 1984)

Husain, Shahrukh A.   *Focus on India* (Hamish Hamilton, 1986)

Jacobsen, Peter and Kristensen, Preben *A Family in India* (Wayland, 1984)

Judd, Denis   *The British Raj* (Wayland, 1987)

Kanitar, Hemant   *Hinduism* (Wayland, 1985)

Kanitar, Hemant   *Indian Food and Drink* (Wayland, 1986)

Kanitar, Hemant   *The Partition of India* (Wayland, 1987)

Kapoor, S.S.   *Sikh Festivals* (Wayland, 1985)

Leigh, Vanora   *Mother Teresa* (Wayland, 1985)

Lye, Keith   *Let's Go to India* (Franklin Watts, 1982)

Mitter, Swasti   *Hindu Festivals* (Wayland, 1985)

Moon, Bernice and Cliff *India is my Country* (Wayland, 1985)

Powell, Avril   *A Struggle for Freedom in India* (Macdonald Educational, 1986)

Singh, Daljit and Smith, Angela   *The Sikh World* (Macdonald Educational, 1985)

Tigwell, Tony   *Sakina in India* (A. & C. Black, 1982)

Warner, Rachel   *Chinnoda's School in India* (A. & C. Black, 1984)

Picture acknowledgements

All photographs were taken by Jimmy Holmes with the exception of the following: The Bridgeman Art Library 10; Chapel Studios Picture Library 41 (bottom right), 44 (top); Bruce Coleman Ltd 18 (bottom); David Cumming 15 (top right); Chris Fairclough Colour Library 30 (top); Hutchison Library 14 (bottom), 24 (top), 32 (bottom), 42 (top); Ann and Bury Peerless 13 (bottom), 15 (bottom), 33 (left), 36, 37 (bottom), 38, 39 (bottom), 40, 42 (bottom), 43; Wayland Picture Library 3, 17 (bottom), 18 (left), 20; ZEFA 8, 9 (top). All artwork by Peter Bull.

Index